- PART 2 -

INNOCENT THOUGHTS

A REAL JOURNEY BUILD JUST WITH THOUGHTS

PRATIKSHA MISRA

ISBN 979-8-89446-077-2

About Innocent Thoughts: Part 2

I hope all of you have had time to read my first book, filled with some of the poetry collection that I wrote and shared for the first time in an offline manner. Now I am about to unfold, not only just poetry from my first book, but also some quotes and thoughts that I keep getting interrupted with while I am deep into the weeds of the hustle and bustle called life. This book does contain all the poems from the first book, so if you start with this book, there is no need to invest your time in the book I published earlier.

It all started when I went on a journey, within myself, and found myself seeking some answers to questions I couldn't either ask or get an answer to. I was abused by a stranger, when I just turned 12, and till date I cannot forget the face of the man, who did that heinous thing to a 12-year-old, who is just trying to understand how her body is evolving every day. That incident broke me and made me think I was better off being a boy, only to my surprise that even boys get abused at a whole another level. Every day I feel, I will overcome the shame that

I encountered, when that man, took my hand and made me hold his private area, in front of my parents? but for me the biggest challenge was unraveling this journey of being free from being ashamed, were not everyone who is abused should be the one victimized, but rather victimizing the society that believes, that such incidents need to make sure that a specific gender gets pushed to be suppressed or be in lesser control than anyone else.

In a phase of me, trying to find answers for each one of you, who is tired of being someone they don't want to be.

In a phase of me, trying to understand the plight of life, where you become someone who is taken care of from its very existence to a person who starts to care about someone else's existence.

In a phase of me when I finally understood what love is, and how it persists until the end but changes at every stage of experiencing it.

In a phase of becoming a mother of a 10-year-old and trying to go back in time to live each moment with your child again, so that it doesn't feel like a bird that's locked in a cage forever.

In a phase of becoming a writer who writes, the emotions that most of us are fighting against, writes for most of us that cannot express it all, even though it's right there inside of you.

Now I am going to leave you to read and explore your own self in this selfless journey of differentiating you from the you that belongs to everyone else.

Don't hesitate to reach out to me anytime with your suggestions and do follow my Facebook Page:" JustUtter", where I publish new posts every day for my 64K followers that hasn't stopped to grow since past 14 years, and a huge thanks to each one of my readers, as I experience to be with such a generous crowd, to learn and converse with on a daily basis.

Feel free to come and talk to me and let me experience the real you via my **podcast – JustUtter**

Or directly connect with me at
"www.pratikshamisra.com"

"I feel you, but what I hear is much
louder than just you."

**All writings are subjected to be solely my collection,*
so please value my thoughts and reach out to me
if you want to share my thoughts or collaborate,
don't just go for a copyright violation.

Contents

Love		**13**
1.	Marriage	14
Walk With You		**17**
2.	In Love	18
3.	Once Again	20
4.	Realm	22
5.	Shades of Color	23
6.	The Way You Looked at Me	25
7.	Choice	27
8.	Indifferent	28
I am		**31**
9.	I Like	32
10.	I am Not Perfect	34
11.	A Writer	36
12.	Foolish	38

13. A Poet 40

14. Selfish 41

15. Who Am I? 43

16. Pretentious 45

Mornings **47**

17. A Cup of Tea 48

18. Every day Is a New Day 50

19. Drew 52

20. Butterfly 54

21. Happy 55

22. Winter 57

23. Drops 59

24. Rain 60

Innocence **63**

25. Drops Of Innocence 64

26. Born 66

27. Darkness 68

28. Inheritance 70

29. Afraid 72

30. Love the Love In 74

31. Child In You 76

32. Motherhood 78

Heartbreak **81**

33. Heartbreak 82
34. Impatient 85
35. Departure 86
36. Sit There Still 88
37. Numb 89
38. Broken 91
39. Illusion 92
40. Sitting Beside You 94

LOSS **97**

41. Grief 98
42. Flowers in My Grave 101
43. Separation 103
44. Loss 105
45. Remember 107
46. Pause 109
47. The Last Breath 112
48. Uproot 115

Fate **117**

49. Success 118
50. Noise 120
51. Fate 122

52. Spear 123
53. Win 125
54. Different 127
55. Dress Up 130
56. Rejection 134

Friends 137
57. Fading Friends 138
58. Growing Up 140
59. Smell Of You 142
60. Dressed Up 144
61. Friendship 148
62. Friend 150
63. Friends I Like 152
64. Metamorphosis 154

Life 159
65. Undo 160
66. There Is More 162
67. There Goes 164
68. Decipher 166
69. Get Into the List 168
70. What Do We Live For? 170

71. Don't 174

72. Try Life 177

Travel **179**

73. The Train 180

74. The Walk 182

75. The Endless Wait 184

76. The Road Was My Own 186

77. Traveler 188

78. The Pictures That I Took 189

79. Nomad 191

80. Into The Woods 193

81. Why Can't I? 195

82. A Special Poem by My Daughter Advika 197

It's the end of a nice old way… *199*

Love

"While we all fall in love,
some wait to be loved by an irresistible fool."

Chapter 1

Marriage

We are innocent, we are shrewd,
We are scared, we are rude.
We are brave, we are coward,
We pamper, we argue.
We give pain, very often we feel the pain,
We lose, often we gain.
We smile, we cry,
We frown, and very often we even behave like clowns.
We love, often we hate,
We trust, we doubt,
We fail, but we often revamp the failure into success.
We teach, we follow,
We steal, and often we borrow.
We fight, we overreact,
We tackle, and very often we tumble.
We support, we shiver,
We defend, we surrender.

We push, but very often we pull,
We force, we regret.
We apologize, we dissect,
We are shocked, but very often surprised.
We respect, we irritate,
We serve, we exfoliate,
And this "we" always tends to depend upon each other in the funniest yet adventurous relationship prevailing on earth called "Marriage".

Walk With You

Hold my hands, I want to walk with you,
Wherever you are headed, take me with you.
I know the path is fatal, but I am not scared,
With you, it's always the break of dawn,
As I hate the fear of you being gone.

Let's go, we can make it to the horizon,
As I wandered where it was.
But when we walked through this quivering sand,
I feel we have reached beyond the horizon band,
The place where souls meet without any magic wand.

I follow you, as I walk with you,
As I want to capture your footsteps.
These steps had led me into a glorified phase of my life,
Nurtured, bloomed, and grew overlooking all the strife.
Being behind can make your fumbles unwind,
If ever you lose me, you can always look back and find me.

(P.S. This piece is dedicated to my parents who taught me the art of togetherness.)

Chapter 2

In Love

I don't remember falling in love with you...
Do remember the wounded sighs,
As you stood with worried eyes,
The grasp gets tighter while you hold.
I don't remember falling in love with you...
Just remember the night,
When a loved one was lost,
You sat there while tears never stopped,
Looked hideous but you never left.
I don't remember falling in love with you...
Just remember the moment,
When people get caught up with reason,
Never valuing the season,
When emotions get skipped,
Soul's tear and flipped.
Falling in love is a chance...
Can happen at a single glance.

Forced to wipe off...
Pulled away from or step down.
But while it lasts...
It paints the whole town.

Chapter 3

Once Again

Once again
we will fall in love
Once again
It will be on a train
Once again
On our way back
I will give you the company
And once again
We will make it rain
Once again
You will rush in a hurry
And once again
I will pull you into my umbrella
Once again
While you smile at me
Once again
those eyes will be what I see

right before you vanish behind the tree
into the house
that happened to have no windows
As I never got to
Find you back.
Once Again...

Chapter 4

Realm

From the realms of muse...
Into the arms you choose.
From the freedom set loose...
Into the times that ceased to exist.
From the realms of nowhere...
Into the eyes that stare.
From the charm of false prepare…
Into the outcome of self-repair.
From the realms of the unknown...
Into the spirited alone.
From the swarm of anxiety...
Into the abode of a petrifying noise.
The realm is beyond you…
The path exploits new.
To abide is your call…
It gets wider than persuade.

Chapter 5

Shades of Color

Shades of color
Bright and blue.
Landed on the branch
Splashing drops of dew.
Through the sparkling water
What I did encounter.
Was a dripping smile
On a leafy pile.
Looking at which
I couldn't switch.
My eyes did twitch
By a feeble crow's screech.
Chilly winds
Turning the woods darker.
Our eyes met
As we stood there wet.
Icy breeze

Cropping to freeze.
Deep wounds healed
As heart ceased.

Stood still
Instead of taking the flight.
As the Shades of color turned white.

Chapter 6

The Way You Looked at Me

While nobody could see,
The hue was as clear as the sea,
Words few but free,
As droplets seek a tree,
The way you looked at me.

Couldn't help but glee,
An urge to get hold of you and flee,
As a goblet filled with spree,
The way you looked at me.

Splashed water, indifferent laughter,
Jolted out a blurry sigh,
Wet beneath the glasses, confronting the horizon,
where one's not supposed to fly.
The way you looked at me.

While I forgot stagnant worries,
Jotting down debacle memories,
That painted poignant stories,
Slowly going out of sight,
Were those eyes,
The way they closed out on me

Chapter 7

Choice

Stepping out at night.
Holding your hands tight...
Hoping you might.
Never be out of sight...
Laughing our hearts out.
A deep urge to shout...
Beneath lie promises.
That never left the premises...
Jumping higher to reach the cloud.
Tipping toes standing proud...
Suddenly hit the ground.
Not bothered by the sound...
Besides the cold heartbeats.
Everything lost was never found...

Chapter 8

Indifferent

Somedays you will tell me your story,
Somedays I will be all ears.
Somedays you will hold me not to leave,
Somedays I will hold my tears.
Somedays you will sing a song,
Somedays I will be wrong.
Somedays you push me firm,
Somedays I affirm.
Someways you will break my heart,
Someways I will keep playing my part,
Someways you will choose to depart,
Someways I will wait before falling apart,
Sometimes you will be there,
Sometimes I won't.
Sometimes it will rain,
Sometimes it will be pleasantly sunny,
Sometimes you will look into my eyes,

Sometimes I will choose to hide it from you.
Sometimes you will walk away,
Sometimes I will be forbidden,
Sometimes we will be coherent,
But in some ways will still be Indifferent.

I am

"If you choose me, don't lose me."

Chapter 9

I Like

Sometimes I Like......

Sometimes I like hiding from myself,
Sitting in my closet where the world can't reach me.
Standing underneath the shower all drenched, with closed eyes,
Without any thought pinching me.
Where I can see only me...

Sometimes I like the poignant shore,
My feet in the sand go deeper, as I feel the waves.
The celestial waves that come rushing up to you,
As wants in our lives when fulfilled, never cease to want more.
Where I can see how greedy I am...

Sometimes I like the hushed sky,
My eyes often catch a glimpse of the bustling clouds,
They blend into each other to form a whopping one.
As our hopes crowd we gradually rise to a lot of expectations.
Where I can see my hopes piling up...

Sometimes I like the little birds chirping in my window,
Gazing at them makes my heart filled with joy,
hopping together in the cherry tree,
Slicing food with tiny beaks among their fellow mates,
As often do we forget to share and spare time for our friends who meant a lot to us one day,
Where I can see the friends, I missed out...

Sometimes I like the rain,
The downpour which makes the splashing tip-tap noise,
Which shuts all other sounds rambling within us,
What remains is the silence and calmness of the water while it touches the earth,
The sight of blooming flowers twittering with their smiling flair,
Where I can smell the simplicity and innocence of the inner me...

Chapter 10

I am Not Perfect

I am not perfect.
No, I am not.
Having said that,
No one is nor ever will be.
You keep thinking about someone,
And they don't.
No two minds think alike,
Not until they dislike it.

I am not a saint.
No, I am not.
My identity doesn't define character,
Nor slaughtering it will make any difference.
I trust strangers.
Yes, I don't know why.
They leave as abruptly as they arrive,
But that doesn't stop me from diving.

I am not evil.
Yet at times thoughts grow twisted.
Staying sober is expected,
But after neglect things fall apart.
I know we are in for a purpose.
Solving others dissolving your cause.
You can't command or request,
Not even make them your quest.
Pleasing to be just,
Easy comes trust.
Until you wait till it ends up in rust.

Chapter 11

A Writer

A writer is alone,
walks home.
With footsteps following,
sleeps alone.
Besides noisy windows,
they get louder when it rains.
Talks to people,
that don't exist.
Makes conversations,
with people from the past
Asks questions,
not wishing for answers.
Gets slammed doors,
for annoying neighbors.
Reads books,
overlooking shadows.
In their world,

they are prisoners.
That gives out symbols,
by writing on walls.
For others to read,
and know what the price is,
of being free.

Chapter 12

Foolish

Nervous laughter,

a perishable chatter,

a silent slaughter,
a devotional disaster,
unheard words,
desirable chords,
a distinct shadow,
an unreleased arrow,
the peasant looks,
a shallow brook,
the garden wet,
the flowers did melt,
naked feet sliding in the grass,
the smell of earth-like rebirth,
clinging quiet,

a solo recites,
chilly breeze,
as life ceased,
an abrupt stop,
a sudden drop,
and I stood still,
against my will.

Chapter 13

A Poet

Poetry is the language,
That conveys,
The unsaid emotions Within...

Poetry is courage,
To fight,
The untold lies
Within…

Poetry is the expression,
That says everything,
Even though relating.
Nothing to harm
The likelihood of one's
Existence…

Chapter 14

Selfish

Our eyes met,
as they were meant,
bowing down relentlessly,
to the priceless gesture,
hands were held,
as our hearts felt.
serving bravely,
to the sacred venture.
selfish as we all are,
painless to the terrible scar,
the forbidden door left ajar,
while minds were at war.
loving yourself instead,
scared to take the step ahead,
paths don't cross,
and no one measures the loss,
the faith is endless,

but what happens next is clueless.
for your life is,
as for life, you are.
the stones leap,
while the flow changes its course.
looking at yourself you weep,
not long as pain eases the source.

Chapter 15

Who Am I?

Is this you or is this just me?
that I am unable to see,
closer to free.
so long on a tedious spree,
tied to the mode,
of self-abode.
Is this who I am or is this who I have become?
hilarious to boredom,
crying silly trying to be free-spirited,
empathetic jargons,
slightly hunched with heavier wagons,
holding hands made of sand,
quicker unwind,
surging blind.

Is this what I want to be?
an incomplete caricature of an unknown stature,

revealing plausible myth,
covered in a colossal sheath,
deeper the dive,
the steeper the climb,
breathing alive yet again,
worried about the future.

Chapter 16

Pretentious

I get tired of smiling at times.

Heart raging with anger but struggling to utter a single word of profanity.

Loved someone till death but that someone couldn't risk his freedom,

Every moment seems to be an illusion as I want to be me but couldn't be. Nobody wants to see the real me...

With despair, I run far away from the truth to pursue harder,

Only to risk my life with loneliness.

Is this what we call life? I live every day as they say.

Carving thoughts out of clouds, singing in the rain, wiping the windowpane, and humming with the birds while walking down the meadows.

Chasing the sunset, splashing water running along the shore.

Lying right next to him talking through the night till
the sun lights up his face.

Knowing days will pass by but no wishes to fear.

Look what I become where wants haunt me and desire
lures me, keeping me on my toes never letting me
breathe the fresh air.

It's not who I am and running just makes this worse

Mornings

"Mornings have learnings."

Chapter 17

A Cup of Tea

A cup of tea says a lot.
Makes me steal a thought,
Or, two.
Takes me through a journey of stories,
Quite a few.
Were conversations,
Made eyes giggle,
Where someone had no clue,
That their morning was slipping through.

A Cup of tea,
On a train.
With the hustle and bustle of
Fellow passengers,
Who were strangers last night?
But now you are wondering,
When will her brother stop the fight?

And when the next stop comes,
Will the boy get his kite that flew right over?

A Cup of tea,
While chasing your baby.
Your tea gets cold,
But you sip it at one gulp,
As you hold her tight
When she puts up a fight
Not to go to school,
As even you don't want to get her out of sight.

A Cup of tea,
With friends in town.
They end up waking up early
And you smell the cardamom flavor.
The chatter gets louder with every sip.
You find it harder to keep away.
From the last tip of the remaining cookie,
While you ask your friend to make another
Cup of tea...

Chapter 18

Every day Is a New Day

Bring that playlist out,
That's hidden in your favorites.
Dust that book,
That you threw under the shelf.
Knowingly play that one song,
That takes you to the times you always belong.
Fall in love with the same eyes,
That once taught you the meaning of love.
Dance slowly while closing your eyes,
With the one who made you dance the whole night.
Kiss the forehead of the one,
Who left you midway?
Dream that subway again,
Where you met this fascinating stranger, with whom you spoke for hours.
Fly along with the friends,
That made you glide,

Saving you from every fall that night,
As you took the drunk plight
Have that long walk on the beach,
Fearlessly running beyond reach.
Hide from everyone but you,
Because every day is a new day.
And you learn to love when you start,
Living it that way.

Chapter 19

Drew

I drew.
A puppet that could fly.
I drew.
A trumpet that would lie.
I drew.
A horse that will not run.
I drew.
It's a course just for fun.
I drew.
I with long white hair.
I drew.
A robber that will not dare.
I drew.
A pauper who refuses to beg.
I drew.
A butterfly without a leg.
I drew.

A sword that feared blood.
I drew.
An angry face.
That would never change its pace.
I drew hope.
That will never win.
I drew desire.
That will fight outliers.
I drew a friend.
Sitting beside me watching the sunset.
I drew hands.
That never leaves me after dark.
I drew night.
Beaming with stars.
I drew faces.
Smiling at me from afar.
But I never drew the frown.
Even when I failed to draw each one their crown.

Chapter 20

Butterfly

In my hand, there's a butterfly,
that doesn't want to fly,
I wonder why,
she goes to my fingers,
her tiny feet soothe me as they linger,
but she doesn't fly,
I wonder why,
I make her sit in a flower,
but she comes back to me,
as I am not sure what she sees...
but she doesn't want to go back,
to what she teased,
as she eases into my hands
while I stand there to
release her into freedom.

Chapter 21

Happy

What Makes You Happy?
A silent conversation,
No words without hesitation,
A hidden smile,
Flattery eyes,
Beyond the horizon seeks the sunrise.

Little footsteps,
Tiny arms holding on unable,
To resist the fall,
An innocent chatter,
Beyond waves the roaring laughter.

Dozing off lazily,
A shoulder drops by,
Giving out a sigh,

Trying harder not to cry,
Beyond the clouds lies the prolific sky.

Tapping on the door,
Peeping through the window,
Taking a glance at the shadow on the floor,
Walking up to the outburst galore,
Amidst trees there lies a path that always takes you home.

Chapter 22

Winter

Frost Bells at My Doorstep...

Dew drops call me out as they peep through my window,
The trees cherish the classy look as the autumn leaves flutter,
The elves uneasy with the freezing outburst
as the frost fairy winks with a twinkle in her eye,
making them all the more shy.

Sun dares to fetch some room through my porch,
as a wedding ballroom with glistening silver adorns.
Glassy alter with luscious green carpet,
Frost fairy seems excited about the divine trumpet.
Not realizing the tear drops all over her wedding dress,
It was the sun if only I could guess.

Mr. Squirrel goes hither and thither gathering bites,
as he realizes the advent of colder nights.
The winter birds chirp their songs comforting him,
While the bugs march to their hideouts,
convincing Mr. Squirrel to engage the warblers.

Just when the ducks fumble their way through a freezing lake,
Mr. Squirrel mumbles "We got the wedding cake..."

I rush in and put on my smiling coat,
as the chilly wind tickled me, I sneezed out laughter,
A freezing whisper of winter surged through my ear.
The blessings had begun as a soothing musical breeze,
when he kisses the bride gazing at them as they freeze.

Chapter 23

Drops

Drops of dew
Glistening outside the window.
A shining quilt gets sewn.
Melting the hearts of few.
A golden streak Followed the charming beak.
Sitting at the tallest bark.
As it starts getting dark…
Falling from the sky
As a squeaky squirrel passes by.
Feeling shy are those eyes.
Which smiles looking as it flies..
Touching your face
Right when it touches his.
Giving out a smirk.
Gathering Droplets at the brink.

Chapter 24

Rain

As the light gets dimmer...

I look out for the birds flying into the dark shining clouds...

Where the sky is free-spirited with droplets of water gushing out

Splashing the earth with eternal bliss...

While here I lay on the grass smelling the dusty wind...

Soaring high I try to touch the smell and sneak it in as if it never ends...

There goes a sparrow discussing his childhood with a squeaky neighborhood.

Bounded by the vows a chariot has come to take the Rain Goddess while she prefers tip-toeing on the wet petals crying on her way as she hates the flowers that withered not getting the chance to bloom...

She flocks into the arms of Earth which makes her shiver, but this is the fearless last time as she closes her eyes and tries not to weep...

On my hands, the trickles seem to be whispering to the grass about the discovery to which wind and breeze cover her back with the jazzy bass...

I tried to ignore it as much, but the trees couldn't stop themselves from dancing to the tune making me wet all over...

They all start showering their best wishes to which Rain blushes...

My eyes get damp while I see her flashing her glistening attire like she is on fire...

When Finally, the Sun arrives to take his Queen, he bows down loyally spreading his majestic rainbow...

Everything gets calm as he brightly makes her shy away...but the pain remains hidden in the darkness of the clouds as they start clearing up...

I wish her adieu so did the Earth...only her heart knows that someday she will fight her way back again...

Innocence

"Sometimes the little steps running towards you make you stronger…"

Chapter 25

Drops Of Innocence

Tears rolled down, Sitting on that bench, all drenched,
drowning already with water all over my face.
Closed my eyes to feel supple fingers comforting my forehead,
Caught up in dreams cause never made any attempt to be dead.

People staring at me as they passed, looks deep diving inside me.
Waking up, I try to find some napkins which can make me clean,
But couldn't help the rain just gushing into me
And drops just poured out like a heavy downpour which was difficult to cease.

"My child you want some hot chocolate", a voice inside me whispered.
It was her, whose fingers I felt earlier.

she was talking to me now. How I love going back to her!!!

Only to realize that there was no going back.

Ahhh!! Why doesn't it stop raining?

Moments after, couldn't help getting that hot chocolate.

Every sip had a drop to trickle just to save my hot drink.

Warmness beneath and melancholy had forced my eyes to dimmer,

fluffy hands seizing me into their enchantment,

slowly losing out on my lament.

Chapter 26

Born

I was born,
for better days,
for sober ways.
For discreet wisdom,
For unbiased love,
For containing sorrow.
To escape tomorrow,
For trapping happiness.
To reflect tranquility,
Did birth answer my queries?
Worn out gets the mask filled with flurries,
Born,
To fear tyranny.
To smear uncanny.
To resist pursuit.

To travel novice.

Right from peeping through the crystal womb,

Until the way into a silent tomb.

Chapter 27

Darkness

Distant words,
An awkward whisper.
Twinkling dishes,
And a sneaky slipper.
The warmth of a mother,
Pain of a smother.
The wrath of a bother,
Hustles from a gather.
Newborn squirm...
Midnight glowworm,
Trapped in a kiss,
Last-minute stitches.
The seamless moon,
With a hidden tune.
A lonely walk,
And troublesome talk.
An unknown sign,

A puzzled line.
Love spelled wrong,
The end stretched long.
Drops dry up,
Felt a knock at the door.
That could be you.
Don't want to go if that's not true.
With heavy knots,
My eyes start to give up.
But thoughts just stare,
Hard to fight flare.
As the dark sinks in.
Beneath the night,
The mind goes thin,
Darkness is mean,
While life turns unseen.

Chapter 28

Inheritance

A little girl loves to watch her frock go swirling in the air,
as she dances to the tune of her favorite pair,
looking at her bunny shoes now and then she hops on the floor,
Her mother can't take her eyes off her,
smiles as she peeks standing next to the wooden door.

A young lad thrilled to get his day off for a fishing spree,
as he gathers bait and grabs the fishing rod from the attic,
A dusty book got his attention, real-time fishing tricks penned down by his Dad as a kid,
wearing his hat now he marches out with a pumped-out chest and a skillful mind,
His Dad gazing through the window as his portrait walks down their courtyard lane.

The power of inheritance is a gesture of pride,

Where eyes start watering inevitably when two worlds collide.

This law of nature can easily turn a blind eye to failure,

As there will always be a moment in the future when standing in front of you will be your stature.

Chapter 29

Afraid

Afraid I have been
To the unseen.
What If It Becomes
An outrageous outcome.

Never I have found
Someone to confide.
But with pride
Have always stepped aside.

Since when do consequences matter
as emotions shatter.
You stay put
But it's never enough.

For The people
You see invisible eyes.

don't pay heed
if you call yourself wise.

Afraid I am
To lose you.
When I fought against
To choose you.

There is a picture
In every caricature you draw.
Your heart has a seizure
And Your brain derives measure.

The road ends
Still struggling with what can be mended.
Afraid to let go
You stoop low.

Being Afraid I See
You Can Never Be Free.
What you need is to Overcome
And embrace Freedom.

Chapter 30

Love the Love In

I love the love in
A mother's touch
A father's eyes
A brother's taunt
A sister's flaunt

I love the love in
A mob's trust in the speaker
A group's belief in the preacher
A child's solace in her teacher
A leader making a path for his seeker

I love the love in
Similar likes among friends
Doing repetitive routines with partners
A sense of strength that reflects from a stranger

A lens of innocence shown by a kid while you shout
back at her in anger

I love the love in
The struggles that life puts you through
The juggles in making something out of nothing
Traveling somewhere without knowing
Taking a long walk to shake the anxiety within
Talking to yourself about how strong you have become
That you finally have started to love the love in loving
none other than yourself

Chapter 31

Child In You

Blowing bubbles.
Popping one by one.
Splashing water.
Roaring with laughter.
Going round and round.
Until you hit the ground.
Rowing innocence.
With simplifying nonsense.
Bowing with gratitude.
To avoid solitude.
Rattling stubbornness.
Fighting keenness.
Hitting the run.
Not forfeiting the fun.
Holding the need.
Never thinking where it leads.
Fearless trip.

And a never-ending grip.
Instant tears.
With wholesome cheers.
The art of discovery.
Ignoring the cover.
Truth isn't trouble...
And lies are feeble.
Your reflection distracts...
What attracts is the child in you.

Chapter 32

Motherhood

A teary eye
With a heavy sigh.
Shadows touched
Deep within.

Feeling the warmth
Right underneath.
Clasping fingers
Sinking soul.
Fear the dawn
When time unfolds.
Pledging courage
Embracing departure.
Sharing tears
With every fear.
Never torn apart
Always very dear.

Tiny steps

Narrating nights.

Tedious fights

Holding them tight.

Walking away into a blurry sight.

Heartbreak

*"You don't leave people for a reason,
you find a reason so that leaving becomes an
easier process than anticipated."*

Chapter 33

Heartbreak

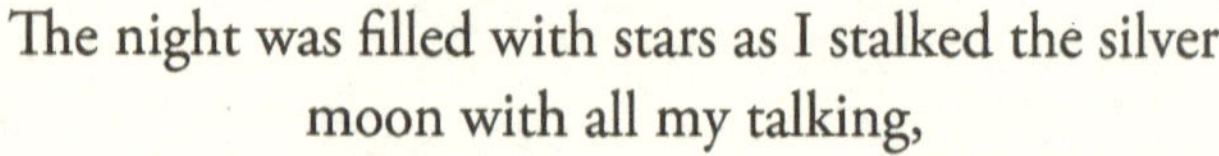

The night was filled with stars as I stalked the silver moon with all my talking,

Caught those angelic eyes on the sidewalk which for a moment blinked as I kept walking.

The earth beneath went upside down where I stood smiling hiding my frown,

That day was worth remembering as the eyes invented an invisible crown.

A deep breath pure in stature making a warm sheath with infinite moments of caricature,

The Smile right in front gives you more than when it's with you,

Addiction is annoying but the way it happens it's without you knowing.

And Here I am Now...

The chilly wind held me tight as my heart had tripped over,
Standing there while he has gone forever,
Drifting apart falling under,
Courageous when you are the one to surrender.

Dragged myself past the same sidewalk,
As my eyes had stopped searching anymore whatever it was, had left me feeling sore.
Fighting the clouds as I felt despised by the drops touching me,
Wiping as I couldn't stop getting wet all over my face,
For destiny had already defined its way to end the chase.

Living in an illusion is where everyone's heart dwells,
The mind plays its games so running towards darkness is lame.

There is a river to swallow along with a mud pit to wallow in,
Others will get chosen over you,
While you stare long enough to be tired of thinking what if it was you?
Opening the door to scornful laughter as you comfort your heart to cease the pain.

There is no truth in love,

What you feel is Lies, when You Tighten the grip It Defies.

The last puff when you quit smoking,

should be enough to last a lifetime sparing you remorse and eternal choking.

It is the Emotions that make the roaring Noise,

But The Heart Breaks With Poise.

Chapter 34

Impatient

A Swollen Heart.
Comes without a statutory warning.
As the grass is wet from the rains.
The more you try not to think the more it pains.
With Corrosive Shiver.
Trembling nerves unable to deliver.
Eyes quiver refusing anger.
The more you try to forget the more it lingers.
Leaving a Holy Scar.
Smelling earth washed by a heavy shower.
You make up your mind.
But what you are best at is rewind.
Never to Surrender.
While walking through the gate.
As I watched my empty fate
Doesn't have to be any longer.

Chapter 35

Departure

Our eyes met,
couldn't help getting wet.
Holding hands,
With carefree words.

Minds made up,
Hearts messed up.
Eyes begging as they kept gliding,
With another of them busy hiding.

Breathing close to,
As Destiny chose to.
Loosing still defining,
Bruised yet aligning.

Making a joke or two,

The parting gates open.

Only sighs remain,

The two smile again.

Chapter 36

Sit There Still

Sit there still...
While someone left abode.
Sit there still...
While there's a subtle erode.
Sit there still...
While inner instances have slowed.
Sit there still...
Sometimes dark clouds fold the boldness inside.
As sometimes weaknesses hide the wrestling ride.
Sometimes being unknown overpowers the superficial glide.
Sit there still...
For now, there will be no change for a while.
For now, there will be no mockery in exile.
As of now, there will be just a colloquial hypothesis.
Along with traces of your wiped-out footsteps.

Chapter 37

Numb

Let a bunch of people break your heart.
Get a crowd to laugh, while you start.
Let a mob muffle you to squeal.
Get an audience trapped under your veil.
Let innocence withstand on its own.
Get bravery engraved in your bones.
Let doors open to coward eyes.
Get people to stare all over your lies.
Let the walls be penetrable.
As strong pillars get vulnerable.
Let freedom lurk.
Silences sulk.
Memories collapse.
And a mere touch becomes invisible.
Stand right there.
As the light goes dimmer.
Barging into the darkest dungeon.

Is the fear left alone?

Conscience pitch black.

Emotions succumbed and were gullible.

You cease defining moments.

Leading your way to the incorrigible.

Chapter 38

Broken

Counted as I picked
The scattered pieces.
Lost my count
As I reached the moment ceases.
Some were sharp
Cutting open a wound.
Deep yet soft
Letting a cry with no sound.
Reasons ponder
Without surrender.
Still, an urge to hold them together
While sorting them out forever.
Hope challenges future
The body starts to rupture.
Slept not to awaken
Falling prey to the broken.

Chapter 39

Illusion

I know what you were going to say
When you looked at me today.
But then waking up to my dismay
It was the piercing sun ray.
There Is a shadow that follows
Even though it seems pretty much hollow.
While falling back on your sorrow
When someone can catch your wallow.

Distance doesn't seem too far
Keeping the invisible door ajar.
While you close your thoughts at war
A journey through the eyes catches the shooting star.
Seeking is not the only destination
Where dreams promise to unfold imaginations.
The one who creates a lasting impression.
Is enough to be engraved beneath your reflection.

Never picture forever
As the journey can end whenever.
Make you embark on an endeavor
Without forcing a futuristic favor.
I knew that you were not going to stay
For you never created an illusion to play.
There is nothing to say
But still, I think what if I may?

Chapter 40

Sitting Beside You

I cannot sit beside you
While you cry.
Dripping drops of tears
Without trying to Stop the smear.
I cannot sit beside you
While you think
As I am afraid
Destiny doesn't seldom blink.
I cannot sit beside you
While you pray.
Wishing all you want
To be yours as you may.
I cannot sit beside you
When there is someone
Already chosen
For you to stay.
I cannot sit beside you

Yet I won't deny
That every day
My promise fades
But truth evades
Engraving it to the last evening shade.

"Love can't hate you,
but it can love you no more."

Loss

*"Some days I feel the same people
are waiting for me at different dimensions
to have similar conversations."*

Chapter 41

Grief

I stood right there but you were gone
Tried holding you back but your presence faded
My head was still resting on your lap when you moved away
My hands tightly in my grasp couldn't avoid the emptiness
Eyes just don't want to believe what they are bound to see
They held their breathe while looking everywhere for the face which lit me up

I stand right across but you chose not to cross
With the thought of meeting you, I doze off
Every day the birds of dawn ask me for your arrival
As the horses run past me at dusk, you are nowhere close

The Moments spent were right here haven't even realized they are bygone

When you heard me while walking along without denying a reply

Like a cloud in an empty sky puffing me as you sway

As the night gets darker I see you coming my way

Holding my hands keeping them close to your heart

I cannot help my tears

My fearless being might get startled by the pain

Hope remains to see you again

While my mind is aware driving me insane

As I smile at you when you smile back

As you hold me never let me go

I run only to find myself trudging through sand as it becomes impossible to reach

My waves are ready to hit the shore but the sun has set

And the tide will soon die down

I don't see this ending

With you self-gone and my thoughts still pending

It will perish once it forgets to hurt

Until then grief might stay making its way out through tears of dismay

Chapter 42

Flowers in My Grave

I want them to be white
Talking to each other in delight
And almost right enough...

To light up faces
While they go down the memory lane
With me while standing tough...
Put a pale tint of red,
As I have said enough...

For things to change
So want to listen as they arrange their thoughts courageously
Marching through the journey
That came through without fluff...

With a flair of orange
Filled with the laughter of kids
Running along making the masses stop crying
as they look over

Don't wear the flowers down
Don't let tears of departure stick to your frown
Through heavy hearts
I would like everyone to have yellow tarts
Eating while their cheeks turn peach
It's right then, I will reach out to each one of you
And whisper a heartwarming speech.

Thanks for coming...

Chapter 43

Separation

A hole in her frock.
What if people mock?
She refused to become the laughingstock.
Coming from a hole.
Dark like charcoal.
Where spirits had burnt.
Squeamish but she learnt.
An unknown path.
She kept walking towards me.
As no one is going to follow.
Looking out for her sorrow.
Whatever she sees.
Will let her be.
And whatever she does.
Must eventually agree.
As hands get annoying.
Faces start lying.

She looks around to find it.
The ones who were there.
Are not even trying.
Is she allowed to be scared?
Stuff until she is layered.
Sometimes she is outrun.
Sometimes she gets caught.
Sometimes she hides behind walls that run paper thin.
Noises reached out to her.
Unavoidably failing to stir.

A loss makes the murmur.
Longing for the road.
Which is back in.
What if she decides?
And gets trapped in.
With only the windows.
Starting at her.
While she wonders.
Is someone out there still looking?

Chapter 44

Loss

I stood there
But I was everywhere
Her smile
Flashing in front
Her gesture
To confront
A faint grunt
With a soft stunt
Someone pulled
To the present
Where I didn't want
To be anymore
The waves roar
All night
Behind the windows
Empty pillows
Salty shoes

That we wore
The last time
We were on the beach
Now alone
Devouring the cone
I stood there
But was everywhere

Chapter 45

Remember

The moment it took, for you to look
horizon Drifting By, melting up the sky.
Nights gulping away
The Moon's Reflection.
There is no fiction
But an honest compilation.
Requesting a last chance
On the very next glance.
Playing the odds
Surpass the winning glory.
Tears wet the story
Dreams portray the past...
Keep feeling aghast.
Memories don't fail
They are forced to quit the sail.
Forget seems inevitable

Those eyes never lie only did shy.

Waves smashed an impatient shore

As The roaring wind cried until sore.

Ashes of remembrance dissolve.

Chapter 46

Pause

Take sometime.
Through the pictures taken.
Through the faces that looked.
So close to you.
Even when you chose not to look at you.
Take sometime.
Through the story trip.
Through the tight grip.
When someone caught you.
Even when you glided to slip.
Take sometime.
Through the games back to back.
Through the knee kick.
Shouting the words that repeated just you.
Even when you were mostly down the stack.
Take sometime.
Through the dreams that got the slot.

Through a dubiously magical plot.
Breathing into the lap while warmth did heal.
Even when you tried hard not to reveal.
Take sometime.
Through laughter.
Through the fights.
Through the moment with the spark.
Through the sadness embarks.
Through the loss.
That caught hold of you crying.
Through the plead.
That caught Moss with you trying.
Through the endless beats.
Through the guardless retreats.
Through passion.
Through the season.
Through the reason.
That wept behind.
Even when you just left right after the find.
Take sometime.
As when you do.
You know what you did or didn't cause.
Do you know what was courage or wasn't chivalry?

You recall the loss.

You gather the cause.

And then.

You take the most awaited pause.

After which you start looking beyond pictures.

Chapter 47

The Last Breath

As I walked past a flower bed of blooming buds couldn't help but smile..

My toes felt the broken strap unable to withstand my body weight luckily getting caught by his arms like the new guy in your life holding you tight enough to not let you go only to realize that the grasp cannot last forever.

The fall leaves knock at my bare foot with a rustling noise notifying me that they will be gone for a while now making sure I will be around the next time they are here..

Two pairs of innocent eyes catch my glance as they try their first kiss next to a dancing gnome...thinking about which caresses my mind as a young bliss.

Never got provoked by the thought that there will be a day when you trudge back all by yourself experiencing a lot of echo due to the emptiness.

Close to my heart is the day his pinkish presence made me cry at the same time my soul had never felt so strong as I designated myself as the protective warrior of the innocent being till eternity..

This made the raindrops flock around me reminding the drenching hours spent tasting those drops before letting them touch my face, as I splashed my way through the sidewalk with muddy shoes and a glowing face..

It feels like yesterday!

The road to my house never seemed so distant enough for me that I would quit running towards the doorstep.

But today it feels so.

Jumping to and fro on the staircase filling my mouth with my favorite pie was my mom.

Will she still be standing there ??

Ahh !!!..the tears show up on my face. You try to avoid them and here they are.

They always come for a reason.

"You have started forgetting stuff", said my grandson yesterday. I laugh back looking at my son who doesn't even feel the need to wish me on my birthday.

It sounded like a car screech on the road making me realize that life should give us the intended jerks as we all get comfortable and used to the speed..

That way when finally people expect you to slow down and pretend withered it will not come to you as a surprise.

The blooming buds still looked at me as the sun started to flare up.

It's time to get up and head back to the long tedious road.

Only to find out that I caught my last breath last night with the fall leaves getting ready for Winter.

Chapter 48

Uproot

Fingers told the story,
Those hands couldn't feel.
Jitters over the story,
Lonely minds would steal.
Hidden behind the veil.
Stood a poetic remorse,
That pierced ceasing a course,
Glitters molded the story,
Those tears couldn't be revealed.
Courage butchered the story,
Where fear couldn't heal.
Uprooted was a glory,
With only a scar to seal.
Fallen guards thereby kneel.
Getting beheaded with steel.

Fate

"Some doors don't open no matter how hard you try."

Chapter 49

Success

There is a path where we all travel alone,
You follow someone until one day that someone becomes a no one.
The light which leads you through the path is a myth,
There is darkness and treachery underneath the sheath.

Sometimes you do the people way and at times the other way,
Until you finally learn to persuade.
You strive for a companion throughout
Even when you find many until
You decide you don't need any.

In the beginning, you kept the account for every step,
After which you heedlessly skipped a lot of steps.
Your pace dragged you into a blind diversion
And suddenly you discover a path of illusion.

You narrow down your ways and the path becomes steeper,

You have become weak and the weak have become stronger.

The journey slows down and the someone whom you followed is nowhere to be found.

Your close associates have sufficed to those who cared for their presence.

You are left out wandering for a distinct essence,

Walking and humming along into another epic of success.

Chapter 50

Noise

All the time
They talk to me
Filling me over
To the brim.
To escape I try
Distractions pry
Shouting on top
To fill the gap.
Always around
Sinking you down
Hidden tears
Taunting fears
Crowded it sounds
By Diving deep
you can only weep.
Eyes are reflection
Defeating perplexity.

They cannot defy judgment
But follow an agreement
The more you see
The more you choose.
Not to lose
Either being empowered by an inner voice
Or ignore it as there seems to be a lot of noise.

Chapter 51

Fate

Dust accumulates.
Trust stimulates...
A Story correlates.
But destiny stands straight.
Faith resides.
Thoughts collide.
Dreaming with open wide.
Your eyes are unworthy to decide.
To the open.
A favored token...
Awaiting Outside.
Grab the ride before it's taken…

Chapter 52

Spear

She will remember.
Your tears.
She will respect.
Your fears.
She will curl up.
Finding you near.
Your daughter.
Becomes your spear.
When you talk.
She will hear.
When you walk.
She will step near.
Your thoughts.
Crystal clear.
With her around.
Your mind.
Resonate steer.

With her very sound.
She will keep you dear.
Even pounded with smear.
Beautiful will she make you.
In your skin.
Warm as she appears.
Traversing through as you win.

Chapter 53

Win

There is laughter in every kill.
And sadness in every shrill.
You hate someone with a heart.
Love fades but hatred never departs.
Waking up with moist eyes.
Are emotions that never die.
A covered wound takes longer to heal.
As pain persists longer than you feel.

There is slaughter in every insult.
And ego bursts following an age-old cult.
You love only to your dismay.
Drinking the potion is not a word you say.
Every day you evolve within.
As sentiments continue to lather.
You try to take the ship much farther.
As memories don't let you think.

Destroying inner spirits in a blink.
Everyone falls in love.
Turning a blind eye to the everlasting dove.
Even if it seems incorrect.
Plunging into is resurrect.
Reality doesn't bother me.
As you hold hands forever.
You enter a pact with Yourself.
Breaking of which is an ugly reflection.
Every niceness is ruined after that portion.
Every defeat is a win.
Every armor is respect.
Only death should make you cry.
Life is how you ride to fly.
Love is power, not possession.
Seek it with no repent over unheard decisions.
Kill every spell insult none.
Trudge with true spirits and bow to The One.

Chapter 54

Different

Normal.., you are right.
You win every fight.
You smirk at other people's plight.
You talk smart.
Making convoluted gestures.
You paint colors.
Disregarding the theme.
Mark faces based on skin.
Snob around the crowd going thin.
Look up to people who peep through windows.
Childishly deferring sorrows.
Acting like the shot dart.
Making the center torn apart.
Faking heartache for spectacular's sake.
You mock weird.
Laugh smeared.

Your reflection coincides.
With no kingdom pride.
But Normal gets forgotten the moment you leave the stage.
Unheard as soon as you try to leave the cage.
The days are the same.
But your words echo lame.
Promises are being bundled into empty carts.
Perhaps the way you end even before it starts.
While Different.
Figures out.
Though mostly in doubt.
Loud noises seem muse.
Doesn't demand or accuse.
Tried at the least.
So what if we lose?
Choose the wrong.
Start again strong.
They snooze.
Doze off.
Stand still.
Wait up.
For almost all the reasons.

Cause being different.

Are you learning?

To canvas out every gradient.

Without giving up silently.

Chapter 55

Dress Up

Dress Up.

Wear your armor.

Dress Up.

To the rumor.

Dress Up.

For Your Battles.

Dress Up.

Not just to Win.

Dress Up.

To uphold disappointment.

Dress Up.

To shield resentment.

Dress Up.

To mourn.

Dress Up.

To be sworn.

Dress Up.

To be heard.
Dress Up.
To be a turd.
Dress Up.
To outshine.
Dress Up.
To have a spine.
Dress Up.
To the valiant bones.
Dress Up.
To be radiant alone.
Dress Up.
To be nervous.
Dress Up.
To be trivial.
Dress Up.
Like the first light of dawn.
Dress Up.
In the vivid colors of dusk.
Dress Up.
Like the free sky.
Dress Up.
To every face engraved in your memory.
Dress Up.

So that every part injects.
A different you as it reflects.
Dress Up.
Like you were just born.
Dress Up.
To the lunatic song.
Dress Up.
As you will never be forgotten.
Dress Up.
For those hands held you.
Even when you were a moron.
Dress Up.
To beliefs.
Dress Up.
To falsehoods.
Dress Up.
To hold up.
Even though your wholesome is gone.
Dress Up.
To act well.
Even if you find it hard to tell
Dress Up.
To weaknesses.
Dress Up.

To solaces.

Dress Up.

In wide grins.

Dress Up.

In Glittered Fins.

Dress Up.

To Outrage.

Dress Up.

To Salvage.

Dress Up.

Bow down.

And look there's nothing to fear..

When you have your dress on.

Chapter 56

Rejection

Step Aside

You have not been picked.
You have not been picked
To play the heroic role in the drama.
Not been selected
To make the audience clap at your poetic charisma.
Not picked in the group.

To march next to the troop.
Your girl says never.
When all you thought was her this summer.
No not picked for the friend's birthday.
Yet asked for a ride on the same friend's wedding day.
Can you please
Do not take the cheese.
Who are you trying to appease?
When what I get from everyone is tease.

Grinning at me all the time.
Don't worry you are sublime.

Stand Out
And you don't get to shout.
Accepting failure with such a disaster.
You can't cry with laughter.
Cause you need to hide.
People love it when you slide.
Bad choices make you num.
Still better than not being picked up by your mum.

Make your Way
Don't wait until today.
Hold the push.
Climb the windy mountain.
Run in the dark with a flickering lantern.
Let people scream.
You scream louder.
Get your feathers greasy.
Flap your wings and fly lazily.
You were picked.
When the coin just flipped.

"Calm down,
as it is not a battle to win."

Friends

"With Friendships Comes the Push of Getting Better."

Chapter 57

Fading Friends

We Don't Cry or Lie.
Don't fight or steal a bite.
Don't hold unless told.
Don't bother to jump in and corner.
Don't pry, Don't try.
Ease to ego and let go.
Don't bake a surprise cake.
Don't take it for old time's sake.
No wake-up to save a breakup.
No questions asked.
What's wrong? Or Can you Hold Strong ?..

Scroll up and down the memories.
But forget all about the stories.

What and How.

Nothing Now..

Stick as long as you don't prick.

Because Friendship fades like an old trick.

Chapter 58

Growing Up

I wonder with the years passing by,
Will I ever be able to fly...

I see the sun the same way,
But the shine feels fading away...

I feel the moon closer to my heart,
And the nights indulging deeper in thoughts.

I try to go back in time to taste the sweetness of lime,
to get to touch my childhood which was glorious and sublime..

I don't want to get worried for the most,
I want to skip growing up at any cost.

Well, there is a way you can,
Don't have to fight with the whole clan.

You live up to what you have wanted,
And then think about what all you wished for was granted.

Looking at it this way isn't that bad,
People always find their reasons to be sad.

Life can never be rainbow-clad,
Sometimes you need to get drenched in the rain still feeling glad.

For pain, it coexists making you stronger to persist,
And Happiness is a myth underneath a shining sheath.

Chapter 59

Smell Of You

Flipping pages of a book brand new.
Breathing in smoke from someone in the walkway.
Catching the train while drenched in rain.
Puffing the wet that instant.
Lying on the grass basking in the winter sun.
Saving all the fun for later.
Innocent flatter.
Unknown chatter.
Trying to hear a voice that just echoes.
A fresh coat of paint.
Not trying to be a saint.
Faint laughter.
A song getting softer.
Fading dusk.
Everlasting thirst.
Water trickles down the brook.
Flowers free falling from the trees you shook.

Snowflake crumples.
Mud base tumbles.
Teardrops on the paper.
The night stars are blurry like the vapor.
Breathless Dawn.
The smiling yawn.
Slept the most.
While dreaming that smell of you

Chapter 60

Dressed Up

I dressed up
For a party.
That I won't be going
I messed
The make up
For a party
That I won't be going
I troubled myself
To get ready
But who am I kidding
I fumbled through the drawer
To pick the right color shade
But there's something lacking
I fixed my hair
Like a messy bun
But I couldn't find the hairpins
Why can't I just put on my slippers

For the party.
But everyone will be looking
I can't tell my best friend
That I fought earlier
She will tell her friend and I don't know
Who else does her friend talk to
I keep walking in my underwear
But now that I am thinking
I shouldn't overdo
If I want to cry should keep crying
I remembered that I promised to come
For the party.
That I won't be going
Why did I do so
Why couldn't anyone ask me not to do that
Just then my phone had a picture of my friend
She looked drop-dead gorgeous
While I looked at the mirror
And seem unconscious
Where did the magic go
I know I can wash off and change
But I went to sleep instead
I called her up
And lied about my reasons

For the party
That I won't be going
I came up with three
I blurted them out as they were free
On the other end
I could sense pity
But I didn't call to sound witty
The lights went dimmer
I wished I looked slimmer
I will eat less from tomorrow
I covered up
closed my eyes as
I found myself dressed up
In red
Looking lean and well-fed
Although my wings
Tossed me in circles
I was lost and found with star twinkles
Until my magic unwrapped
Me asleep deep in a blanket
Filled with wrinkles.
The dream wasn't bad
So I let it go on with chuckles
At least I had a party

Where I was glad I had dressed up
Even though I hexed up
I wasn't obsessed
To nuances
That leads to obscurity.

Chapter 61

Friendship

Close your eyes.
Rest your head.
As you find the shoulder of a friend.
Sit back.
Track the sun.
While it sets.
As by your side.
Sipping coffee is a friend.
Laugh louder.
The voice getting bolder.
Echoing amidst the crowd.
Peeps a friend.
Cry childishly.
Turning nose red.
Rolling over the grass bed.
While lying still next to you is a friend.
Thinking of them.

Ballistic overwhelm.
As dreamt of flame.
That fire in you is a friend.
Departed.
Forgotten.
Hiding behind days.
Where once upon a time was a friend.
Nothing can be it.
Replacing a heartbeat.
Waiting all night on the street.
Sitting in a room filled with heat.
Changing to be upbeat.
Tears of joyous fleet.
Just to see you are a friend.

Chapter 62

Friend

How often do we think about our friends?.... We don't usually think about all our friends, there is always one special friend, with whom you let go of all your troubles, your happiness as well as your sadness. It's difficult to find such a friend in your lifetime. But some are lucky to have them, and they cherish this friendship more than anything else in this world. I even have a true friend of mine. This person influenced me a lot, at first, we hardly used to get along with each other, but as we came closer, we used to like each other's company. We both used to be ourselves when we used to talk or meet up. To date, we have been the best of friends. This thought came to me back in 2005, when I was in college. In 4 years, we both became great friends, from worst enemies. This Innocent Thought.... for you my Wonderful Friend then and now my husband for 14 years.

Whenever I close my eyes, I see you, my friend,

as a shoulder on which I am leaning.......

Whenever I am troubled, I search you, my friend,

as a shadow in which I can hide away.....
Whenever I am sad, I need you, my friend,

as a tree to shower my tears on.....
Whenever I am happy, I want you my friend,
as a cake to put the icing on my happiness....
Whenever it gets dark, stand close to my friend,

as a burning flame through which I can see my path...

Whenever it gets lonely, be there my friend,
as will hold your hand while walking...
Whenever it gets rough, be there my friend,

as with you facing the world will not be tough...
So Dear Friend, I owe you a lot.......

God grant all the wishes in my friend's wish pot....

We both need to go a long way.......

I Promise to Be with You Everyday

Chapter 63

Friends I Like

I like the friends
Who sit tirelessly
Waiting for you
Being sure that
You would come
As you have promised to do so
No matter what.

I like the friends
Who supports you?
In front of the world.
Even when there is
High chance that
The world will leave them
For doing so

I like the friends
Who cry?
The moment they see
Tears trickling
Down yours

I like my friends.
Who tell me
They are angry
And still
End up hugging you still
As their will
Has made up their mind
To be with you no matter what

Chapter 64

Metamorphosis

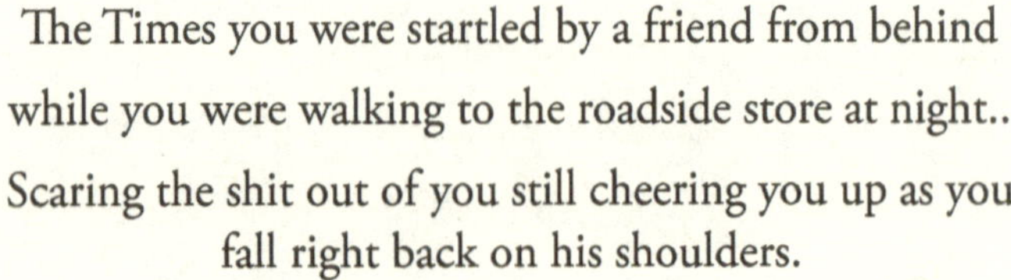

The Times you were startled by a friend from behind

while you were walking to the roadside store at night..

Scaring the shit out of you still cheering you up as you fall right back on his shoulders.

That essence of trust that no matter what he will not let you fall..

The Times you got drunk and went home sheepishly..

Only to realize all but you are stupid enough to be happy with the fact that "They Don't Know"

When every single one was aware as you kept stinking the whole night with the weird "Mint With The Alcohol Combination"...

The Times you passed on your answer sheets at the finals.

having the dragon heart to make your buddy get through.

While the headmistress stares at you scribbling on your rough sheet

to crack the code.

Phew !!..That was close.

The Times you are at war with your folks..

who are polite enough to say "You are always Wrong".

but the moment you face betrayal you unknowingly say "Damn Why Are They Always Right".

The Times when you push your friend when he proposes to your girl.

and the very next moment you pat on his back saying "You Can Have Her.."

The Times when you just messed all up badly.

But still, you are at peace when you come home and close your eyes

Only to find yourself on your mother's lap

With your father screaming loud enough to let the neighbors peep through their windows.

The Times when you are told, shouted upon, insulted, laughed at, loved for, pushed back, pulled in.

Somewhere the realization was just as a mirage..

Now

While walking in the dark makes me fear Loneliness.

I check on my drinks even before we get started.

Don't recall any friend so close to my heart anymore...

Miss my folk's interference.

Always constantly pushing each other like some kind of rat race.

So long since I closed my stressful eyes and found myself sleeping on her lap.

And If you mess up this time you are on your own.

This is where I am at when I am neither asked nor suggested any options.

There is no one to hold me and grab me into doing what is right.

But I tell you those Times taught me a lot and are still worthy enough to bring a chuckle to my face.

I may not be marvelously winning this race.

I may not be fulfilling some great expectations.

I am proudly living each day of my life as I cherish those times

For One Fine Day, I transformed from being carefree to the one who was willing to say.

"I Care...

Life

"The irony of life is it always changes when you have made up your mind to stick to your comfort spot."

Chapter 65

Undo

Undo the ties.
The unwanted lies.
Undo the whys.
The unending cries.
Undo the chapters.
With well written ever afters.
Undo the ladder.
Which goes backward.
Undo the words.
That pulled you down.
Undo the hope.
With a hardwired rope.
Undo the knot.
Tweaking the plot.
Undo the charm.
Before it does any harm.
Undo the thoughts.

Undo the slots.
Undo the moments.
That fetched happiness.
Undo the sight.
Undo the fight.
Undo every right.
Undo that you might.
Undo the weirdest night.
Undo the strangest delight.
Undo the sunset.
Undo the offset.
Undo the click.
Undo every trick.
But while
Undoing the clue.
All you ever knew.
There will be few.
That will never be undone.

Chapter 66

There Is More

Behind a shut door,
Inside an empty store,
Between the pieces tore,
Beyond the pompous shore,
There is more.
Underneath the laughing roar,
Tripped out a hidden tear.
Filling up an outrageous air,
Climbing down the rusty stair.
There is more.
My heart went sore,
Or A soul driven tour,
Eyes turned sour,
Or A ripped-off core.
But still, there is more.
Never left before,
Walked out the door,

Tears touched the floor,
Standing there ignore,
Memories riving galore,
Yet there will be more.

Chapter 67

There Goes

There goes.
A life without definition.
There goes.
A goal without determination.
There goes.
Dreams that ignited.
There goes.
Imaginations that subsided.
There goes.
Love which was trust.
There goes.
A friendship which was a must.
There goes.
The Scars healed.
There goes.
Hidden people revealed.
There goes.

Arguments that never got over.

There goes.

True spirits which were ram over.

There goes.

The pity filled with a soulful touch.

There goes.

Selfless humanity with an unstable crutch.

There goes.

The scattered topography boarding is a painful philosophy.

There goes.

The only friend.

There goes.

A legitimate offense.

There goes.

Believe.

There goes.

Deceive.

There goes.

Everyone turned blind.

Towards a world so unkind.

Chapter 68

Decipher

To whom,
To what,
To where,
To go,
To stay,
To be fair,
To love,
To wish,
To declare,
Whenever,
Create,
Modify,
Decipher,
Look out,
Stay put,
Jump on.
On the edge,

Who matters,
In the end,
Who shatters,
Over the crowd,
Who finds,
Among the shout,
Who whispers,
Through the darkness,
Who holds,
Through the tears,
Who scolds,
Witness the moment,
Travel the sentiment,
Capture the lament,
A constellation of emotions,
Where happiness wouldn't last,
But struggle pulls you back at last.

Chapter 69

Get Into the List

You are in someone's todo list
In someone's do-not-call list
In someone's friend list
In someone's trend list
In someone's top of the list
In someone's invisible list
In someone's trust list
In someone's betrayal list
In someone's can't do without a list
In someone's never list
In someone's try list
In someone's why list
In someone's hold-onto list
In someone's let go list
In someone's angry list
In someone's sorry list
In someone's guest list

In someone's waste list
In someone's waitlist
In someone's late list
What matters at the end
Is that one list
Where you made it without pretending
That's the real list
That got the real you
Despite knowing the twist
That you come with
Despite knowing the mist
That you shower when
It's a bad day to live with
But that list has you inside out
Without the simplest doubt

Chapter 70

What Do We Live For?

I am worried,
don't be,
you don't see,
what I do,
I see it,
but tend to ignore,
Why do you do that?
because I don't want to know,
that we are walking towards Hollow,
we are following shadows,
we are marking empty spaces,
we are tracking invisible footmarks,
What are you talking about?
again, I don't want to know,
so even though I know, I don't,
doesn't it bother you?
It does, but I choose the other one without bother,

while one calms down,
I become the clown,
while one is out of town,
I wear the crown and sit on a throne,
made of plastic stone,
these riddles are making me sick,
that was the plan and now it did the trick,
Which one should I pick?
You know you think too much,
there is nothing called choice as such,
A mother doesn't pick her kids,
A farmer doesn't pick the land,
An animal doesn't pick its dwelling,
An orphan doesn't pick its parents,
there is a simple equation,
you do the things that bring emotions,
you do the things that let go of frustrations,
you do the things that you are meant to do,
being as simple as sitting and saying nothing,
watching a game that your team is losing,
rooting for a kid that's rising and falling,
the sun does that too,
the moon follows along,
there is nothing right and wrong,

even criminals do sing a song,

jails have humans that haven't been able to process anger,

whales eat animals that they don't even know suffices their hunger

What's your point?

I don't know, and I don't want to know.

if you are going for that play,

let me dress up,

if you make up your mind not to,

I can get into my nightgown and sit on the couch,

sip a bit,

wink a bit,

until I doze off...

It's been a long conversation

Let's practice silent communication

Let's practice spontaneous artwork

Let's practice speaking our hearts out

Let's practice treating everyone equal

Let's practice going out on the streets and greeting everyone

You need to stop.

Okay I will

But I know you got the message

Well, all I know is that this is a passage
Where we travel to go beyond
What we live for in its entirety
Is not to lose ourselves in this tornado
Of reality...

Chapter 71

Don't

Wait for,
it was never meant to happen,
Don't
plan out,
it's never going to happen,
Don't
think too much,
you might choke yourself.
Don't
feel awful,
that's life move on.
Don't
hope death,
It will come and you won't even know.
Don't
search happiness,
It's right there inside you.

Don't
be too down-to-earth,
unless you want to be squished into a muddy pit.
Don't
smile until you want to,
as you make someone's last wish.
Don't
Regret said and done,
that was you and this is still you.
Don't
hate yourself,
everyone does so you better don't.
Don't
love anybody and everybody.
that just happens and it's filled with remorse.
Don't
sacrifice because you are not immortal,
but do it if your heart is hell-bent.

Don't
listen to everything you say to yourself,
it's just a battle between who you are and who you don't want to be.
Don't

pull yourself from what you signed up for,

we all are made of steel,

you will never know unless you stretch it till the very end,

you will never break,

cause that's who you are.

Chapter 72

Try Life

Try life,
for some time.
and then you,
make it rhyme,
until it turns to slime,
or truth fails to chime,
shout it loud,
hold it proud,
avoid the crowd,
Take it to the top of the cloud.
Try it until
you have seen it all,
Try it until
you refuse the fall.
take the dip,
lick the sip,
make it a trip,

while you whip.
Try it steep,
Try it deep,
Try getting creepy,
but do dare weep.
never skip,
nor flip,
never shy,
nor cry,
always try,
to defeat why.
and don't let death,
take your breath,
just hold on,
as every moment.
is born.

Travel

"The traveler spirit is finding your soul in peace no matter what, no matter where."

Chapter 73

The Train

It looked,
as if this was the last train,
I would catch it.
as I hopped in got attached.

Took out from my stash,
a folded piece of paper,
drew the view that eyes could snatch.
while the journey began,
beyond the glorified hatch.

People whose eyes met,
some days running getting wet.
a glimpse of the sun set,
or traveling towards a dark covet.

Walking towards,
waiting for it,
through the crowds,
that lit,
similar faces did fit.

Chapter 74

The Walk

Walked a long way without looking back,
as the chase stared longer,
traveled miles away without an ask,
as breathless monger,
into a never-defining path,
followed an unknown wrath.
A sudden cold breeze
turned his back.
everything visible
was gone.
The arms widespread,
The smothering shade,
The prolific outburst,
The incandescent thirst,
shut out,
Through the soundproof door.
choking to talk,

as he had started to walk.

Chapter 75

The Endless Wait

On the bench alongside the railway tracks,
he had turned his back as trains kept passing by,
the moments spent with her going back and forth in his mind,
It's just that this wait is endless, never to be left behind.

While the waves crashed on the rocks,
birds flock through the empty sky,
as the little girl runs towards the sunset,
looking for tiny paws running back to her,
where only the dusk knows fate never defers.

Getting darker,
she sits sticking her ears to the door,
As the never-ending downpour,

just like the day before,
making the windows shudder,
with each hour echoing louder.

Chapter 76

The Road Was My Own

Into the forest,
as I walked,
The trees looked down at me.
I could see,
My feet are chasing the ground.
soul stretch,
was the naked sketch.
of voices that surround,
the unsaid words,
that I never heard of,
was a fleet filled with birds.
childhood hugging,
falsehood bugging,
left inside,
was the sweat trickling below,
trying to sort narrow,
but forever shallow.

defining virtue,
over needy leaves,
tiptoeing into dry crumple,
stumbled on a stone,
while thunder erodes,
refusing the turn,
as my eyes got wet,
took the wrong road,
that I went alone,
was my own.

Chapter 77

Traveler

I write about people I met,
about people whose eyes went wet,
about people who meant something,
about people who let go of everything,
I write about places I visit,
that talk to me,
that walk with me at every step,
that stalk me as I sleep,
that provoked me to find them no matter what,
I write about free spirits,
about the dancing street,
about the glaring little girl,
about the forest that fumes with fire,
about the mother who doesn't sleep,
about the man who smokes to forget,
about the morning that holds you,
about the night that folds you.

Chapter 78

The Pictures That I Took

Looking at his shoes,
a kid waits.
chasing ants on a bench,
stars on his trench,
lonely eyes at the gate,
just before the sun sets,
a girl rushes through heavy rain
with an umbrella,
as her shoes splashes water in the narrow lane,
checking her watch,
if she is late,
a whisper in her ear,
after which a smile appears,
dense clouds,
beneath the moonlight,
crowded streets at night,
two friends walk,

the same way they talk,
as kids in a relic plight,
dogs chasing shadows,
hunger peeping through windows,
snow-covered roofs during winter,
sitting by the fire soaking in warmth,
bits of ashes swarming,
drops of tears staring right through,
train arrives with a glance at someone,
insane eyes searching for no one,
change in color,
while dawn meets morning dew,
change is captured,
when gone sweeps startling new,
all the pictures that I took,
can never be well described in a book,
you got to see what they make,
out of life that just fails to shake,
when you start to look.

Chapter 79

Nomad

She reads books, exchanges looks,
as she enters the land of freedom,
likes every part of what she has become,
compares with her past,
and falls in love with the contrast,
away from the appalling crowd,
following the direction where clouds take her.

as a nomad,
she chases every train,
sits next to strangers,
talks like a foreigner,
her mood resonates with a daydreamer,
until the journey comes to an end,

after which she is back in a body,
of a native dweller,
from the place she once came to visit,
as a lost traveler.

Chapter 80

Into The Woods

Naked and puffy,
wandering in the woods,
stuffed with grass,
troublesome and crude.
knocked out by the breeze,
as the wind whistled and teased,
slapped by the branches,
for my interlude,
trapped in the ignorance of elude.
the night smoke slicing through my eyes,
as the moon lighted up the skies,
a quaint wanderer invading peace,
tracing footsteps of animals walking at ease.
A whimsical tune of darkness persists,
while I caught the whiff of wet earth,
filling up an addiction unworthy to resist,
I ran to dive deeper into the brook.

following the psychedelic crystal ripple,
only to find what all I felt lay in a book.
and me very much inside,
This box is full of people.

Chapter 81

Why Can't I?

I am scared of dying alone,
I am scared of crying to my very bone,
I am scared of hands that detach,
I am scared of any familiar touch.
I am scared of sleeping alongside no one,
bothering to wake me up,
I am scared of meeting no one,
Who would ask me to stay over?
I am scared of trying harder and bending,
surprisingly turning into a dead end.
I am scared of closing my eyes and waking up,
into a room full of strangers.
I am scared of tears flowing down my cheeks that are unstoppable,
I am scared of words that mean nothing,
I am scared of promises that always fall out,
I am scared of happiness, which is short-lived,

I am scared of innocence not so meaningful anymore,
I am scared of hidden stories beneath deep eyes,
I am scared of lies covered under pretty faces,
I am scared of politely killing someone,
I am scared of kindness withholding wrath.
I am scared of anger struggling to pounce on it,
I am scared of smiles that I will never again encounter,
I am scared of life just slipping away from my fingertips,
sweaty hands dampening grip,
Why can't I save anyone by the end of this trip?

Chapter 82

A Special Poem by My Daughter Advika

When she strolled along the beach, and looked at the moonlight, she couldn't resist writing this piece. Follow our **Podcast:JustUtter,** for more of her work.

The moon is so bright,
I see no other light,
As it shines on the seashore,
My footprints I see so faintly,
As my toes dissolve in the sand,
I think to myself,
I would rather not leave this land.

"A Journey Needs to End to Begin Again."

It's the end of a nice old way...

Of getting goosebumps.
It's the end of a pathway.
Filled with yellow blossoms.
It's the end of an essence.
That took your breath away.
It's the end of childishness.
That was swiftly accomplished.
It's the end of a surreal surrender.
With little words to squander.
It's the end of an imaginary effect.
With the magic squared away sooner.
It's the end of the knockout moments.
Prolific emotions.
Gone with a single poof.

Thank You for coming alongside me on this journey….

Poems & Quotes By:

Pratiksha Misra, Author & Publisher of **JustUtter**

www.ingramcontent.com/pod-product-compliance
Lightning Source LLC
LaVergne TN
LVHW041208150826
845673LV00001B/334

* 9 7 9 8 8 9 4 4 6 0 7 7 2 *